Ballet for Adults

the

Physical and Psychological Benefits

Robert Brassel

author of *Always a Dancer*

Robert Brassel Instructs Class

Ballet
for Adults

the

Physical and Psychological Benefits

RESOURCE *Publications* · Eugene, Oregon

Resource Publications
A division of Wipf and Stock Publishers
199 W 8th Ave, Suite 3
Eugene, OR 97401

Ballet for Adults
The Physical and Psychological Benefits
By Brassel, Robert
Copyright © 2008 by Brassel, Robert All rights reserved.
Softcover ISBN-13: 978-1-6667-6799-5
Hardcover ISBN-13: 978-1-6667-6800-8
eBook ISBN-13: 978-1-6667-6801-5
Publication date 12/20/2022
Previously published by AAD Distrubting, 2008

This edition is a scanned facsimile of the original edition published in 2008.

Dedication

To Suzanne Dimpfl,
for taking the first step...

Contents

Preface

A retired ballet dancer in need of exercise finds a local health club that has, among its many exercise rooms, a dance studio with mirrors and barres. The year is 1995.

Ballet class is not a part of the health club's daily class schedule. Was this room ever used for dance? Further investigation offered some answers. Tai Chi and Jazz dance lessons were being offered at the club along with Yoga. Ballroom dance lessons had also been given. Mind/Body classes existed; however, THE basic warm-up class (Beginner Ballet) was missing.

It did not occur to me that it might be a novel idea to start a ballet class in a health club. What did occur to me was the need for ballet training in a setting where so much high impact training was ongoing. A beginner ballet lesson would be the appropriate way to train people in the proper manner of warming up before working out.

The Beginner Ballet lesson, with its centuries old method of developing coordination and strength through proper body alignment exercises, would be a perfect fit in this environment. And so, after a few "back and forths" of a dance between the club management and me, it was decided that we would add a beginner adult ballet lesson to the club's class schedule. We would see if it were a perfect fit. One thing was certain: it would be the way for me to return to a facsimile of the physical condition I once had.

Former professional ballet dancers exercise differently than the general population. At least those of us who go on to live long lives after dancing don't run marathons, walk/run quickly on rolling rubber or lift weights to maintain our condition. In fact, after retirement, it takes some time to even feel that one needs to get involved with the process of maintaining one's physical form. Much of the ballet training is maintained longer than one might presume.

There does come a time, however, when one begins to feel all of one piece: that dreadful joining together of both sides of the muscular structure that is the exact opposite of what dancers know as *opposition*. This sensation of opposing forces in the muscular structure is what gives alignment and balance to the steps ballet dancers execute. It also produces the dancers' "look" so admired by the general public.

Inherent in the ballet training exercises, known as a ballet lesson, is the curriculum to isolate the right side of the body from the left, the top from the bottom. This creates the continual stretching of the body in four opposing directions, N/S/E/W if you will, which produce, in a gradual manner, the grace and posture unique to the ballet dancer. Thus far, no common calisthenics routine has competed well with the ballet class. This gradual warming up of the muscles is missing in other forms of exercise.

When thinking in terms of presenting this method to adults, it is important to remember that the ballet class was designed for the development of the eight-year old's growing body. Could one partially partake in the ballet training process at a later, perhaps much later age? Could one experience something of the fully-formed ballet dancer even though one started late? How late is too late?

The greater question is whether adults, with developed mind and body mass, could discipline the mind in order to achieve a facsimile of what the ballet dancer achieves. For the answers to this and other forthcoming questions to be identified, the adult condition would have to be tested in the ballet class environment.

Applying ballet discipline and decorum to the class would be essential for honest, realistic results. An adult teaching adults would need to keep the focus on the work and not on the individual conditions brought into the lesson. It would require uninterrupted concentration as a collective goal for an extended period of time. Furthermore, a specific adult ballet curriculum would be necessary in order to safeguard against injury.

Finally, in the culture of the "electronic revolution," one realizes that the need to concentrate on one thing at a time has become increasingly difficult. It has also become increasingly important. Taking ballet lessons could be one means of re-introducing adults to the act of discipline, to a sense of concentration over an extended period of time, to a feeling that they are in control of their concentration.

I could only imagine what the results would be for those who regularly ventured into the Sports Club's "Studio B" for lunch hour ballet with Bob!

"To learn is to
be changed."

Lesson

"Shoulders over hips, legs together, try not to slouch even though you are sitting down. Keep your legs turned over and your breathing even. Flex your feet and stretch your feet, relax your head completely toward your feet but do not pull on your legs for greater stretch. Return to full sitting position opening your hands in front of you and then to the side. Now, with your hands overhead but not behind you, turn your torso to the left and then to the right, always keeping the shoulders over the hips and the breathing even. Return to starting position. Repeat."

"Now, with the legs open as wide as you can while still keeping them turned over, flex your feet and stretch your feet as before, relax your head completely toward the floor, keeping the legs turned over. Return to upright sitting position and bring the right arm overhead and the left arm in a circular shape in front of you. Bend this position to the left side and then, changing arms, to the right, keeping the shoulders over the hips. Relax your arms. Repeat, closing your legs together as you finish."

This is the start of the beginner adult ballet lesson. The students are sitting on the floor. The music is a compilation of various ballet lesson compositions put together for this particular lesson level. The terminology used by the instructor is French. At the end of the one-hour lesson, the first-time students will be given a glossary of ballet terms, written in French with English translations and a brief biography of the instructor.

"Please stand up, heels together, shoulders over hips, hips over feet, heads relaxed and breathe evenly." The class is in full concentration. For the remainder of the lesson, their combined effort will be on maintaining proper alignment (shoulders over hips, hips over feet) while executing basic ballet positions and steps. The concentration required will be the most impressive part of the student's lesson experience.

Afterward, the students will discuss the beauty of the music and the calmness required to feel that one has made a successful effort at achieving that which is requested of them. The discussion will then turn to the instructor's unique ability to teach them the rudiments of the art of ballet training. Mostly, they will have experienced an elevated level of proprioception (the sensation of comprehending and coordinating the physical positions of ballet with their limbs).

Instructing adults exclusively for the past thirteen years, I have come to realize that what I do primarily, is help them to stand well in order to improve their posture; alignment, if you will. With that realization has come the understanding of the importance of the curvature in the human spine and how to lengthen and strengthen the muscles controlling that curvature without attempting to forcefully straighten it.

I have come to respect that curvature and to keep my eyes closely on it. In fact, my focus has developed to the point that I am totally concentrated on a person's back and have identified it to the individual long before attempting to remember his or her name. Some embarrassing moments have occurred over the years when I have repeatedly erred in calling the individual by the incorrect name after they first appear in class but I have never confused an individual's back.

Proper body alignment causes a chain reaction throughout the body's musculature: the appropriate muscles go into play, supporting the skeletal structure without needing to ask the person to use certain muscles for the same effect. Oxygen and blood flow increase naturally for maximum energy flow. As a dance student I often heard "pull-up" or "tuck under" from an instructor aiming for proper body alignment. Standing correctly, with shoulders over hips, hips over feet, eliminates the unnecessary verbal commands made by many teachers.

I believe all instructors have their own concepts that they wish to impart. With a professional background in what you are instructing, this should develop gradually to the point where one is certain of the means in which to achieve desired results. Though not all instructors can afford to instruct one level only, success has its best chance if the individual consistently instructs the same level.

Learning the peculiarities of that level and working with them regularly, one becomes refined at what it is that works best. Changing levels will interrupt the development of the instructor and shortchange the class.

Acquiring physical strength requires routine repetition. In addition to repeating desired movements for this result, it is as important to do the exercising on the same day of the week and preferably at the same time of the day. If one swims on Monday of each week, jogs on Tuesdays, does weight-training on Wednesdays regularly, in a routine manner, certain desired results will occur. Change the day or time of the routine or the routine itself, and the results will be less desirable.

Here the sense of doing more, multitasking for the sake of getting enough for one's effort and money, takes over. In our current culture, man seems to have an increasingly more difficult time making decisions in order to choose the best method of working out.

For the adult ballet class, I set one hour lessons on alternate days. This is the best schedule of routine for the optimum results without injury. It is intended to be the lesson one does first before moving on to any other activity. We have seen, collectively, that the best results have come to those who do not overwork the activity schedule and maintain consistency. Being that the place of instruction is a health club, this concept is easily challenged with cross-training opportunities.

Once the Club's management saw that the Wednesday, 11:30 A.M. ballet lesson was a success, adding a second lesson was discussed. I was working the lesson into my workday schedule, using lunchtime. My available time for a second lesson was Friday, 11:30 A.M.

"Oh, that will never work! This is an affluent community, many people take three-day weekends." Well, I needed to place the second lesson at that time for a couple of reasons. One, my schedule allowed for it and another is that alternating days was my goal in setting a schedule of more than one lesson per week. Interestingly, if those who crowded the Friday class took three-day weekends, they took the lesson beforehand. The management of the Club was now more impressed with Adult Ballet Class. The class size was nearing twenty-five on a regular basis.

As the classes grew in number and size, I gradually introduced the new curriculum that I had devised for this particular setting. Picking and choosing what to give to adults on a regular basis while adhering closely to the basic ballet lesson structure, I finalized the curriculum to amount to about one third of the full class curriculum generally given during the training of young individuals.

The results of the first six months were very encouraging. Those who were able to be consistent in attendance were seeing a difference in their general well being: hearing from friends about how well they were carrying themselves, while they themselves were noticing that the amounts of Advil and visits to the chiropractor/orthopedic specialists were down considerably. They were experiencing physical improvements to match the enjoyment of their psychological benefits. Their comments, usually after the lesson, were very gratifying and encouraging to me. The new curriculum, tailored to their 30 to 80 age group, was working well.

As the classes continued during the first year, the curriculum unfolded. Not only were the Friday classes begun without sitting on the floor as the Beginner Wednesday class did, the same or very similar combination of exercises began to take on a slightly quicker tempo, some inversion forms were introduced and a sense of cardiovascular workout could now end the class with beginner jumping exercises.

It wasn't long before faces began to appear in the widows of Studio "B." The curiosity was palpable. I was told by the front desk personnel that the comments from the would-be members having a tour of the club went something like this: "You offer Ballet here?" then, after peering in at the class, "Well, all those people have the same arm up and are using the same foot all at the same time. I would never catch up!"

It was clear that the future members of the club would not be served without the addition of a third lesson, one focused on "new beginners." Looking over my work schedule, Mondays, 12:30 P.M. would have to be it.

Management was happy to add yet another lesson. I felt that we then had the right amount of lessons for the curriculum and that the entire spectrum of interested club members would be properly served. It was discussed with management that an evening lesson be offered for those who could not make the lunch hour ballet time slot.

The lessons would now be graduated in the curriculum, offered every other day of the week and set the pattern which, to this day, has not changed. Over the years we have seen the desired results and we have maintained a safe environment while expressing the educational and spiritual (Mind/Body) enlightenment that studying an art form offers.

We have learned that no age is too late to benefit from this endeavor, that more and more people enjoy the mind/body exercise experience and that, with this particular training, all would repeatedly learn how LESS can be MORE. Ballet training had made its mark in the health club industry and was here to stay.

Tendu à la Seconde à la Barre

The Real Thing

Why would adults be interested in taking a ballet lesson? The reasons I have heard over the years fall mainly into three categories:

1.) to re-acquaint themselves with something done years earlier
2.) to have another chance at that which was prematurely ended
3.) to realize a long-held interest.

All of the above are valid reasons but each differs greatly in the psychological arena and all are based on love for the art form. Thus, it was important to clarify why one was there and what would and would not be the end result of the experience. We would not be producing performers, there would not be pointe work for the women and there would not be choreography as part of the class.

On the other hand, it was important to give authentic ballet technique in the lesson, not a hybrid of class work designed for a health club setting. In other words, adults should get the "real thing." Regarding the French terminology and class music, the adult ballet lesson would be the same as traditional lessons. This had already taken hold throughout the country's ballet schools/studios and now it would enter the world of the heath club industry, bringing the opportunity to those who may not have joined a ballet class elsewhere:

Carol and Joyce-

Two of the earliest members of the class were also two of the loveliest ladies I have ever met. They were also among the oldest members, each sixty-five years old at the time. One, Carol, was a dancer all her life though she did not take the professional route. She brought along to the lesson, Joyce, who had never taken a ballet class but was very interested (category three) and a superb athlete who ran marathons into her sixties. Both had their respective work ethic.

Carol was mainly interested in keeping well through continuous training as she was performing with an elder dance group at the time. Joyce took to ballet as she had taken to other physical activities: something akin to a vulture! Their shared enthusiasm for the class and my presentation of it was very encouraging.

In fact, as Carol began to hone her technique and get some long lost questions about ballet answered, Joyce was

14

so taken by ballet that she began to write poems and draw water colors of everything she was learning in the lesson. For her, it was the artistic outlet that her sports-related activities did not provide. The different psychological benefits that these ladies derived from ballet lessons were founded and clearly evident. That they would both be responding to ballet technique depended upon the "real thing" being given in the lesson. Carol and Joyce were at the opposite ends of the training spectrum. Everyone who followed fell somewhere in between Carol and Joyce but all would be given the "real thing."

Suzanne-

"My father didn't encourage me in my efforts to be a successful ballet student," stated the fitness manager of the club. "I think my lessons were cut off too early. I'd like to take lessons again," she concluded. This is an example of category two. I was beginning to see the value of ballet lessons in broader terms than I was accustomed. Adults were a very different breed of students from adolescents. A different importance was coming into play.

Charlotte-

"I have taken hundreds of ballet lessons but I never really knew the names of the steps, the five arabesques or the eight positions of the body. It is really wonderful to learn it now!" said Charlotte, the newest member of the Club who had transferred to the area from the midwest.

Charlotte, thirty something, was a clear example of category one. Her comments are common remarks from people trained in the United States, a country still without a standard ballet curriculum for teachers.

Until those of us who were trained by various versions of ballet instruction can go to a source where we learn one common method, we are merely continuing the varied processes in which we were instructed. Therein lies the gap-producing training that would cause such exclamations from the "Charlottes" of the ballet class world.

The overall instruction of American dancers has been good. Over time, it has improved and, through trial and error, eliminated major gaps in training. The current efforts within the dance world to formalize a system, whereby one can receive a pedagogy degree is most welcomed. Finally, we may see this come to fruition. Until then, dance training that is safe and inspirational is a good place to start. That includes adult students.

"*Dancing aligns us all.*"

Relevé in First Position

Healthy Alignment

Again my eye caught sight of a red-turbaned head straining to peek through the window into class. She was still there at the end of lesson. I went over to invite her in. I had noticed her inquisitiveness over the previous few lessons but she had never stayed long enough for me to speak with her.

Jane-

Well under five feet tall, quite hunched in stature but with gleamingly bright eyes she inquired, "Do you think I could come into this class?" Only if you promise to wear that wonderful red sweatsuit and turban you have on," I responded. She smiled, standing just a little bit taller. "Have you ever taken a ballet lesson?" I asked. "I was the

Waltz Queen of East Boston 1927!" "Well then, I am sure you will do just fine in this ballet class."

Jane was eighty-seven years old and had recovered from her fourth heart surgery (a quadruple bypass, she told me). She had her doctor's permission to join the health club and her husband agreed as long as it did not interfere with their sailing together. Before we set up a schedule of Monday classes for her, I informed her that the motto for the class was, *to do what you feel you can, leave if you feel you need to but, for all concerned, do not be late to the lesson.*

Jane represented the far end of the class spectrum. At the other end was thirty-something Christine from Ireland who was not yet the Waltz Queen of Lexington but showed fine aptitude. If these two women could benefit from the class instruction, it would be clear that any age could also benefit.

All the members brought their "physical baggage" into the lesson. I understood that, even if there is a perfect physical specimen for a ballet lesson, certainly there is some type of injury, ache, pain, etc., in adults of all ages. The specific class curriculum was prepared with this fact in mind. That said, it was Jane who was about to remind us that, even at an advanced age, the miracle of rhythm was the key to successful movement to music.

She was not a Waltz Queen for nothing. With her left hand on the barre, she did her best to execute the simple plies and tendus. She was quick in addressing corrections, especially those of alignment. Mostly, her movement was always musical and her breathing was relaxed. It was this musicality that was nearest and dearest to her heart and set a special example for others to follow. Working within her capabilities, she saved herself for what she hoped would be a waltz or two in the center of the room. I believe those waltz combinations kept her returning to the lessons, at least for the period before her fifth surgery that would bring an end to her waltzing days: Doctor's orders, "No more ballet lessons for Jane!"

My work on proper alignment seemed to be the reason people returned to the lessons. Many have told me they were now feeling improved energy. Good blood circulation and flow of oxygen are benefits of proper body alignment. An overall feeling of improved well-being continues to be the recurring comment.

The feeling one experiences from being properly aligned with shoulders overs hips and hips over feet is that of being a bit "too" far forward. This is primarily because I instruct that the weight of the body is over the middle of the feet (foot, if on one leg at a time), rather than resting onto the heel, which one is inclined to do, or being too far forward on the metatarsal portion of the foot, which is what taking the instruction too literally often produces. Still, it is quite forward, indeed, from the medical diagram one sees in doctors' offices (the one with the skeleton seen from the side view). Positioning the lifted, slightly tilted head and breastbone in the upright and forward position completes the alignment.

From this properly aligned stance, the anatomy stretches in the four directions as the movement commences. When properly aligned, one is always ready to rise on the balls of the feet. Herein lies the best possible stance and posture for good health. It is what one should be striving for when walking or sitting. Though the spinal curvature must exist for one to be able to walk, lengthening and strengthening that curve is the business of the ballet-aligned stance. What dance class members do is "dance" the stance: their movement is aligned. Alignment is the most important physical aspect the instructor of ballet can instill.

Adults learning ballet offer uniquely challenging choices for the instructor. Developed minds are one thing. Developed strength, often offering an aggressive approach to movement, could prove to be disadvantageous for working the body with ease and grace. Until that strength is aligned, the instrument will continue to beg for a better, an easier way of working gracefully. Ballet exercises answer many of these questions with significant results

One question that comes up often is the correct placement of the lifted chest. Here the properly aligned stance can actually be set backward when the apex of the breastbone is lifted. Instead, I ask that it be lifted and brought forward, along with the remainder of the trunk, at the same time. One of the few images I use in instruction is that one has a string attached to the apex of the breastbone and the other end of the string is attached to the ceiling about ten feet in front of the stance, leading the movement. This enables the breastbone to be lifted without sending the weight backwards.

Alignment also begs the difference from being well placed on one's legs to the trunk of the body being somewhat uncomfortably forward of the legs which I refer to as the "dancer's stance." There is a sense of work in the latter and not in the former. This "work" is referred to as working "well," not "hard," and the difference between the two is nothing less than graceful movement with relaxed breathing.

The "dancer's stance" removes the stress of standing improperly while maintaining the all important, natural tension needed to move well. When we sit down, we keep the tension in the "up" position, usually holding onto the chair arms so as not to fall into the seat. Likewise, on getting up, we keep the tension "down," again holding onto the chair arms so as to get the trunk balanced onto the feet (note that we do this action subconsciously: a natural movement).

Further, my instruction regarding alignment continues with the concept of lifting upward when one is bending the knees (plié) and, likewise, pressing down when rising onto the balls of the feet (relevé). Keeping the alignment while using the aforementioned concept (up to go down, down to go up) becomes ALIGNED DANCING as the movements are put together in a smooth, musical fashion. This becomes the look of the ballet dancer's training, separating it from any other training and yet making it identifiable in any physical activity: walking, sitting, standing still (which we think of as a kind of movement in and unto itself) or on a ballroom dance floor, a ballet stage or reaching for those cereal boxes at the grocery store. It is all physical movement that can be done with alignment.

How often does one feel uncoordinated, or indeed clumsy, when executing the natural workings of the human skeleton? Even the best dancer has had his or her moments of physical uncertainty. Having appropriately tuned musculature at all stages of the life cycle is akin to having resources at one's command; resources we need and use throughout our lives. It is of particular pleasure to offer such resources through ballet lessons and to know that the results are altogether happy feelings.

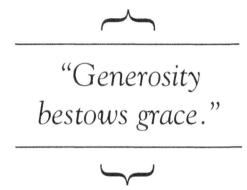

*"Generosity
bestows grace."*

Dégagé en Avant à la Barre

Grace

The wonder of human movement need not be admired only in the young. What woman or man has not admired graceful movement in peoples of all ages? Who has not seen a person dancing gracefully and not thought that person beautiful?

Given the inspired design of the human form, it is evident that naturally endowed human beings are innately graceful. Poor physical habits, allowed to develop from a young age, will impede naturally graceful movement. Practicing a system that develops such movement can improve overall health in mind as well as body. This is what dancers do for a living.

Exercises given in a ballet lesson replace stress and strain of general workouts. Over the past decade we have learned that Mind/Body lessons, given in the health club setting, have surged in popularity. People grew tired of forcing and pushing their muscles and minds to reach their "limit" (one of the many "rewards" of aging.) This, all in the name of "cardio" exercise, is an appropriate metaphor for not really knowing how much is enough.

The acceptance of Mind/Body lessons, beginning with Yoga, indicated that between the average work day and workout, people needed to find a balance and a way to feel balanced. As the electronic age has developed, this need has increased. Our unspoken need to slow down has a way of presenting itself, regardless. It is nothing less than self survival for much of today's population.

Aging is the final reward. With it comes a number of realizations; that perhaps running for hours on pavement is not in the best interest of the mind or body. Was pumping more and more blood through the heart ever a part of the big picture? Does intensity really create a longer life quality? Was that degree of euphoria really necessary?

If one were to use half of his developed strength to execute a movement, one would then, naturally, find a degree of grace present to actually do the movement more easily. Less is, indeed, more. The fear of failure needs to be replaced with the experience of success. To achieve this one needs to practice; be encouraged with reminders and thereby change a gradually disabling habit into a new behavioral pattern that benefits the aging process.

Yoga, Tai Chi, Ballroom Dancing and, more recently, Pilates, all offer the development of grace in their lesson plan. The inner peace and meditative aspects of these disciplines have been the catalyst to their continuing success.

What came before? When did Man first experience grace? Was there anything beside movement that he experienced along with it that motivated his being graceful? Movement was Man's first activity; rhythm, coming from his heart beat, was his motivator.

In the ballet lesson, we simultaneously open our two arms before us (first port de bras). The generous quality of this gesture is thereby gracefully expressed and signifies from where all movement originated. Interestingly, it comes directly below the area of the body that contains the heart of the giver. Giving is one of man's more important psychological needs.

After some months of taking adult ballet lessons regularly, one finds oneself smiling more, looking forward to the next lesson with ever-increasing enthusiasm. One's life was being enhanced and changed by the experience. Being in control of the body's shifting weight; the bending and stretching of muscles, ligaments and tendons and feeling that control motivated by the rhythms of music is to enter a place that everyone would want to visit.

Working gracefully with this most remarkable instrument can be an enlightening experience. As witnessed over these years, with numbers sufficient to make a fair assessment, the adult ballet class is its own validation.

Third Position Bras Couronne

Posture

The interesting thing about posture is that it is most often considered to be a person's physical stance. I think of it as an indication of a person's mental state. How easily we can decipher when a person has a problem; shoulders droop, eyes are unfocused and the overall posture of the person is slouched and the gait is often slowed. Conversely, when the problem is being well managed, the person stands taller, looks another in the eye and moves at a normal gait. Body language speaks very loudly.

Though ballet training produces the physical results of good posture, it cannot make the student use their training to always produce good posture. What ballet training can do is support the physical body when the mind is in less than optimum working order. Sufficient training will come into play on one's worst day.

Many class members have remarked about the enthusiasm they feel when waking up and realizing that today is "ballet lesson day." The subconscious reacts to the elated thought in several different ways but it is the posture that suddenly takes hold in the hours before the lesson. This sense of getting to a place where they can take care of themselves elevates their being.

The students come into the studio with their posture already working! Mentally, they have a very good chance of having a wonderful day. I liken this to the difference between one born into wealth (those who have ballet training early in life) and those who create their own wealth (those who discover the training as adults). Once it is discovered, it is seldom lost. The training has that level of importance to those who practice it on a regular basis.

How often one finds that he is not sure what it is that may be causing lethargic behavioral patterns to form. He doesn't see himself getting into patterns of behavior that cause poor posture. It is common to refer to the aging process as an explanation for any and all negative physical developments. Indeed, there is truth to that reasoning but there are always other factors that come into play. Often the external factors in one's life become slightly out of control and that has a snowball effect, reflected in behavioral patterns that are physically damaging. Our current "multi-tasking" culture plays a large part here.

One way or another we manage to find what it is that we need in our lives. In managing this search, we do so mostly with an eye toward the "easiest" way possible. This common instinct creates behavioral patterns that more often than not require rectification, using the "harder" way.

Having learned the lesson by working the harder way, one often reverts to looking again for the easier way. A new behavioral pattern is long in the learning and longer still in the practice. Repetition is our saving grace here. The technique of mastering beneficial physical and mental behavioral patterns is the great gift dance instructors offer.

In adult ballet lessons, posture is an ongoing effort to "present" well. How one handles oneself is largely due to the appearance he gives to the beholder. Aging can defy the will to handle oneself as well as one used to do. Training that addresses this issue helps to keep posture "still there" in one's daily activities.

I had the fortune of being gifted with impressive posture. It brought me attention and admiration and certainly gave me confidence as a young dancer. Because of it, I appeared to be a more trained dancer than I actually was. For that reason, in the various venues where I auditioned, I was taken "on" often before I should have been. I spent a great deal of time developing my technique to match my posture, particularly during the early part of my ballet career.

For all of that, it was Posture that opened all the doors to my chosen future. I only needed to validate the opportunities with an equal amount of work in order to become the dancer I eventually became.

"He who stands well is clearly heard."

Retiré à la Barre

Focus

As our world has changed and our culture developed, I have noticed over these years a general lack of focus in everyday behavioral patterns. The overall lack of concentration during a conversation and the sense that one is not really listening to or looking at the individual they are interacting with has struck me as increased pre-occupation.

I attribute much of this to the relationship one has with the computer monitor. Personal interchange is experienced in a new manner; an offshoot, if you will, of what is now called "multitasking." We still have a large percentage of the adult population who will need additional time to connect the personal interactions between the computer and the people. Interestingly, one sees how this follows onto the performance stage of today. The performers generally lack contact with the audience. Indeed, this overall lack of focus pervades the citizenry at large.

I know the value of focus in everyday activities, of performing well one act at a time. I am grateful that I have the ballet teaching through which to remind myself and the class of the importance of focusing on the matter at hand. A ballet lesson demonstrates this very well.

"Your lesson is better than therapy. For one hour I can not think of anything but the work of the moment," is a common quote from numerous class members over the years. Certainly, they have to leave the thoughts of their morning, and what will be of their afternoon, at the door. Their problems are not brought into the studio. We do, on occasion, discuss matters of their individual lives after class but while we are in the studio, it is ballet that they are focusing on.

Focus is the single most difficult discipline to master when one is executing ballet exercises. I request it of the beginner student and also remind those who have taken ballet lessons over the years. I consider focus to be the key to learning well and to successful execution; feeling you are in control of your work. Focus is the most important psychological aspect of my instruction of adults learning ballet. It is when one indicates that they were or have been focused in a movement, then repeats it with the correction in place, that I see the learning process in action.

We know that if one were to practice focusing only three hours out of the one hundred twelve waking hours in a week, the results would be slow in coming. Additionally, the movements done in a ballet lesson are unlike movements one makes during all those other waking hours. The objective is to take the ballet training and gradually apply it to daily behavioral patterns. How one walks, sits, shops and stands during the day can be done with alignment and focus or it can be done without.

I imagine that the benefits of ballet lessons can be compounded if they are not left in the studio. I imagine all members of the class working just a little bit on their alignment throughout the day. I imagine that the true sense of well being will ultimately depend on how well one moves throughout the waking hours.

A teacher is a teacher is a teacher! What he teaches is more important than how he teaches it. We know from the world of politics, science and the performing arts that, if a system is thoroughly founded, the chances of success far outweigh those of failure.

This would be the mantra for all who want to transfer information to others. It must be foremost in the priority of what motivates the teacher, before ego itself. I surmise that a teacher is one who observes the differences around him, utilizes his chosen system as a means with which to collect and rectify those differences, and thereby improves the lot of others. Such a teacher is able to be repetitive and patient.

Of the many people who comprise the weekly ballet classes that I instruct, the majority talk with me of the profound sense of satisfaction they feel from taking the lessons. Some feel they have enough just in the music. Others speak of the French terminology that brings them the extra sense of doing something "important." Still others tell me that the manner in which the classes are presented brings about all the elements of the learning experience. And then there are those who have never said a word but speak to me through their newly refocused expression. All are more in unison with the world. Their feelings of having "found" something: of being less fragmented, of better organization between body and mind, of having the guidance of a teacher who maintains belief that his chosen system has resulted in continual return visits to the lessons and the spreading of the word to others.

The lessons have, over the years, become a kind of community unto themselves. Naturally, this seems the common result whenever groups of people convene on a regular basis. Add to this an art form as the common reason for convening and the communion of the group magnifies. For me, that speaks to the value placed on the lessons and the choice of a system well presented and practiced. It also speaks, I feel, to many people's search for a means to a more focused life.

"Fully transferring the body weight one step forward, led by the focused eye, is to know the power of physical authority over motion."

"Inspire the
inspirable"

Community

"You know, the people in ballet class really care about one another. One doesn't feel that in many of the other classes. One doesn't even know the names of the other students half of the time and they barely speak with one another. In ballet class, we really care and learn about one another."

This statement came from a long standing student who has been a member of the Club for many years and cross-trains daily. I asked her if she had a reason for the close camaraderie she felt in ballet class. Searching for the exact wording she wanted, another student standing close by chimed in, "It is the nature of the art form!"

And so it is and has been in ballet schools and companies the world over. For all the competition involved, the sense of camaraderie is palpable. Firstly, there is the caring. Then there is the feeling of participating in a very special

41

activity. From adolescents to the aged, those working together and consistently in a physical art form create a psychological attachment to each other. It is an inclusive experience.

As a group, we have enjoyed parties outside of the class as a means of social interaction. The members are in regular contact with each other and as the class grows in number, so does the friendliness; a sense of contentment supported by physical well-being. Though the community trait is common to the class members, there is the occasional response to the lesson that is exclusive; where one takes the work very personally and keeps their "sacramental" feelings private. Overall, it is a communion in the real sense of its own community.

We have all seen the elevated interest in Mind/Body group exercises. Having something to discuss about the lesson afterward is unique to these type of lessons. There isn't much to talk about after spending one's time on a treadmill.

Further, during this era of electronic communication, banking, shopping, etc., the time humans have together has become more scarce. The need to be together and learn about one another reminds us of the degree of importance we should place on any activity that brings people together.

Social dependence is a positive aspect of life that people have learned to gradually deny. Having a place to be that combines the social issue with the exercise issue seems more essential as time marches on. Any group gathering in schools and studios around the country experience much the same camaraderie as I have discussed here. In the health club setting, with its vast square footage and large membership, adult ballet lessons have found a very natural and welcoming, larger audience.

As the number of students has grown, I remember those who, along with Carol and Joyce, were there in the beginning of my work at the Health Club. I also look at those who later joined the class with an eye toward how they have fared. Their continual comments are, by and large, the inspiration for this book.

Due to their individual tenacity and perseverance to be well and to live well, they have seen the consistency of their activity pay off in various ways:

Dolores-

"More forward?"

For Dolores, about the same age as Carol and Joyce, ballet lessons were new to her exercise regime though she knew something about it and even had incorporated the artform in her artistic work. She was not in good physical condition when she joined the class. Her physical condition deteriorated quickly. In a short time, she was only able to manage stairs if she walked down backwards. Though the pain in her knees was increasing, she continued to do what she could in the beginner ballet lesson.

Finally facing double knee replacement, Dolores maintained her physical routine until the time of her surgery. Though her routine encompassed other instructors that were also monitoring her weakened physical state, she regularly corrected her alignment in class, taking corrections as best she could.

With surgery successful and therapy completed, Dolores returned to all activities of interest with appropriate degrees of success. I know that the ballet training served her well in the years before and after the "new knees" and that the replacements allowed her to resume taking lessons, always working on her alignment so as to be well and therefore, to live well.

Susan-

"WOW!"

So commented the affable Susan after her first ballet class with me. In her late forties, Susan was a formidable physical specimen to encounter. She had been an ice skater early in her life, going on to all outdoor activities. I would say she was an all-around athlete. She became fascinated with ballet lessons and the challenge they brought to her.

Her life changed radically when she had a severe bicycle accident and was as near to death as anyone I had known. Susan was nearly gone by the time she arrived at the hospital's emergency room.

Over several years of therapy and loving attention from her devoted husband, Susan has regained parts of her mental and physical abilities that were thought impossible. She returned to class briefly, but with only one side of the body to work with, she realized that ballet class was not something she was going to do again anytime soon. But who knows, she could walk in one day and surprise us with both sides of her body working again. Her recovery has been that miraculous.

Both Dolores and Susan have given credit to the ballet training and the courage they took from it. In ways not easily quantified, the spirit of the ballet offered them some-thing "extra" when push came to shove. Their posture was their presence.

Having a chance to rediscover or to finally experience a long lost interest is the commonality of the class members; the love of the dance is the common denominator. How that expresses itself and what that means to the individual varies in as many ways as there are bodies and minds at the barre.

Dorit-

"I will always keep trying."

Shortly after meeting Dorit at a local Master Class which I taught, she began to attend my lessons at the Club. Becoming interested in my understanding and instruction of alignment, she also asked me to work privately with her daughter who at the time was a young ballet student. Educated as an architect, Dorit brought a unique sensibility to her work in ballet. Furthermore, she had been trained in ballet as a young person and was returning to it on a regular basis.

Architects know about line. Dancers know about line. The interesting part of instructing Dorit is, as it has been since she first came to the class some twelve years ago, to re-address her sense of line to suit classical ballet while respecting her own particular style of movement. She brings out the architect in me!

Elaine-

"My husband knows how important ballet is to me."

Elaine, a student of dance since the earliest age, has a personal connection to me. She began taking ballet lessons as a first grader along with another little girl who I would one day marry.

I know her dance background very well. She grew up to become a nurse and had been gradually returning to ballet training. My lessons, at first, offered a particular challenge; her schooling was stylistically counter to what I was teaching, though, in fact, they are fundamentally similar in many ways. Different port de bras, numbered arabesques or unfamiliar numbering of the walls and corners of the room were probably the only things Elaine would have to get "used to." Here was a very well-trained dancer who reminded me just how long that fundamental training stays with you. She has been a valuable resource for the other members of the class and, on occasion, I have asked her to substitute teach for me.

Kathy-

"I don't care how long it takes...."

She came into the new beginner lesson seven years ago in a very fragile state of mind, in tears after the first exercise. As she tried to compose herself, I asked her to come back when she felt better.

Clearly, individual problems brought into the class

would have to be addressed. I knew that the work of the class superseded any problems or issues that students might bring along with them.

I later learned that Kathy, in her forties, had more than one physical problem she was dealing with and still more personal problems that were exacerbating her current fragile state of mind. It was her physical therapist who suggested that she take my class as a next step in her rehabilitation program.

I would have to think about being a part of a rehabilitation program. I was not used to that in such a literal manner. When she returned to class, Kathy was composed through most of the session, breaking down before the end. She began to explain some of what she was experiencing in her life. I quickly decided that her therapist was probably correct in suggesting ballet lessons with me.

If she needed to be composed to take a ballet lesson, taking the lessons could only enhance her development. It worked. She took a noble, no nonsense approach to the training and has improved remarkably over the last seven years. Steady as she goes, her consistency has created a work ethic that also helps her to better manage her particular life challenges. I admire her perseverance and determination.

Linda P-

"Do you really think I am a natural dancer?"

From the onset twelve years ago, this painter of vivid colors and technique brought her sensibility for painting to ballet lessons. Hers is a natural grace which is evident even though her attendance can be wildly sporadic. That she finds my assessment of her mystifying further proves that the freedom of expression through movement is not something one can turn on and off.

Tammy-

"I'll only be away ten days!"

A tapper who knows the value of ballet lessons, Tammy brought her natural rhythm to ballet in her first lesson. She is a performer with a local group and maintains her ballet schedule nearly as rigorously as her tap lessons and rehearsals. Interestingly, when a serious interruption in her good health caused a long period away from dance, Tammy did not miss a beat when she returned. Her belief in and trust of dance training sustains her.

Linda M-

"Nobody looks quite as good in a hat, any hat!"

Having quite a lot of training before joining the class ten years ago, Linda is one of the most consistent members of the class. Her interest in dance and dancers is the foundation of her long-held respect for ballet. She has a large knowledge of ballet which supports her effort in learning different ways of doing familiar steps. And she knows a good hat when she sees one!

Ellen Beth-

"I love your class!"

A dancer's dancer, Ellen Beth is an inventor and writer by choice but a dancer at heart. She also teaches other dance and exercise classes at the Club and occasionally finds her way back to ballet. She brings movement experience to the lesson along with her unique sense of dancing enjoyment.

Fred-

"Fred Astaire and Gene Kelly really knew what dancing was all about!"

A retired engineer, Fred became a class member after having been introduced to ballet by another teacher. In his case, this was a godsend to help him rehabilitate from years of playing tennis. He took to ballet in a big way and quickly learned that it is the root of all dance instruction.

As was his manner, he began to research ballet and instructors via the video market and the internet. His consistent attendance has been very impressive to the other male members of the Club and I think a source of inspiration to everyone. For Fred, ballet lessons have given back to him a quality of movement and helped to rid him of pain. On most nights Fred can be found dancing at a club or watching Fred Astaire on video, just to reconfirm what he is already very sure of: dancing is miraculous.

Karen-

"I am going to get it right!"

    With a college dance department background, Karen had little understanding of ballet lessons as something she had mastered. Through the years, while raising children and fighting certain health issues, her inquisitive nature has held her in good stead for mastering more than she thought possible. She has been very consistent in her attendance habits, learning and retaining what she needed to fill the gaps of earlier training.

Merry-

"I hope you can articulate what it is you do in order to achieve what it is you achieve in teaching ballet."

    This comment came from Merry after learning that I was about to embark on writing this book. Another Club member who has a background in dance, mostly modern with some early ballet training, Merry is a psychologist who found my adult beginner ballet lesson to be revealing. She was happiest to be learning the answers to some of her long-held questions, not only about ballet lessons but movement in general and specifically about the connection between ballet and modern dance training. Our conversations about that are ongoing because for so very long the two techniques were considered to be at opposite ends of the movement pole, without due attention to the fact that dance is dance is dance!

Rong Lu-

"I give up promotion so I can come to ballet lesson. It's so important to me."

A research scientist, Rong Lu is certain that she could have been a dancer. She has a deep admiration of the art form and she only misses her lessons if she is in Asia visiting family. She exemplifies what one can learn and execute as an adult learning ballet.

Carol B-

"Oh! I don't think I can do it!"

An accomplished sculptress with a wonderful spirit, Carol brings her artistic sense to the ballet class. Her very early dance training comes shining through in the sure approach to rhythm that she always demonstrates. The lessons have reconfirmed her belief in the way she continues to develop the learning experience.

Shayna-

"I know that ballet class helps my skiing!"

Shayna began her ballet training as an adult with another teacher who happened to be a mutual friend. It wasn't long before she added my lessons to her schedule and showed what lovely spirit lives in the graceful movement of her arms.

She is a reminder that the art of dance is in the upper body. Through the perseverance of a champion, Shayna takes on every challenge the lesson offers with the confident attitude of one who can try almost anything.

Marcia B-

"I like to ballroom dance, too!"

She has the focus required of all good learning and the consistency of a disciplinarian. I am captured by those two qualities for I teach them in each lesson. So goes the positive experience Marcia gets from each and every lesson she takes, ballet and ballroom.

Marcia S-

"Thank you, thank you for giving us such joy!"

Marcia has a wealth of dance training behind her and even more love of it. Her vast experience reflects her life's efforts to learn and be a part of all things that are great. Her ability to improve continues to astound her. However, it is she who reconfirms for me that improvement is always possible.

Diana-

"When I wake up and realize that today is ballet day, I feel so wonderful."

A former instructor of different physical disciplines at the Club and elsewhere, Diana is all about the music. Though she learned the rudiments of classical ballet long after she was an exercise instructor, her confidence and successful mastery of the lessons come directly through her musicality. She is an example of why people like to dance.

Annie H-

"I can't believe it!"

Annie says that often and it exudes her love of learning dance among her sports activities. She retains the ability to be wowed and that pushes her to new levels on a regular basis. A retiree with no prior ballet training, Annie's response to lessons always reminds me how mind-blowing ballet can be.

Donna-

"What have I done now?"

A natural mover with little training before joining the ballet class at the Club, Donna has discovered a passion for learning Classical Ballet and "getting it right." She uses what she learns in her other club activities, everything centering around the dancer she is.

Christine-

"Dancing. I just love it!"

About that lass from Ireland who had the aptitude (page 20), well, she is fulfilling it wildly, madly and lovingly in every lesson she takes. Christine is an Irish Step dancer who began her ballet training with me seven years ago and, through days of trials, learning that class requires discipline, has committed herself to serve ballet before the self; a good example of all that ballet lessons offer.

Leslie-

"I just love your instruction!"

A former dancer and teacher of dance, Leslie joined the class four years ago. She has had a vast amount of training with excellent teachers, knows everything I am teaching about as I teach it and moves like an angel. She is a major asset to the class and the others so enjoy watching her move.

Ann R-

"Amazing how these people keep returning lesson after lesson!"

Ann is another of the few class members who was a trained dancer before beginning lessons with me. Her extensive background manifests itself in more than her technical proficiency; Ann has the discipline of a professional dancer. She belongs to that select group in class that offers others something to reach for.

Babs-

"You make my day!"

Dancing from a very early age, Babs returned to training a couple of years ago when she first began taking my lessons, long after having become a grandmother and a tennis player, teacher and coach. Her enthusiasm and sense of rhythm remind me of the dancers from the vaudeville era; a sensibility that is sorely missing in many of today's professional performers.

Helena-

"Thank you for being so patient with us."

Using her former training and love of movement to work with the very young, Helena joined the class two years ago. Her continuous interest lies in comparing the impetus of movement between modern and classical training. As time moves on for her, she is marrying the two in her own unique manner.

Mia-

"You create such an atmosphere of giving in the room!"

Mia is the newest member of the class but one with a most solid, thorough early training. Although she has not taken lessons for many years, her work of seven continuous years at an early age immediately proves the fact that somethings never really leave you. It is going to be very nice to have her around.

Ami S-

"Bravo Maestro!"

It's as good as the grand bow she displayed when I ended the lesson one day thanking her for saving the day by providing music when mine was suddenly lost. Ami returned to ballet lessons as a wife and mother who had a lot of early ballet training and a great love for all things theatrical. I might add that I think we are on the way to finding her true sense of relaxation in ballet.

Judith S-

"I come to the lessons because I love ballet!"

After a long career of working with young people in the summer camp setting, Judith is living her life to the fullest with grandchildren, travel, ballet lessons and more travel. Her spirit for dance is an outgrowth of her true love and appreciation for the artform.

Mary-lu-

"I am learning so much!"

With some prior training, Mary-lu joined the class about two years ago. She was very happy and surprised to find ballet lessons at the Club. Within a short time and with excellent attendance, she has shown confidence in her work and a greater authority in her movement. Her approach is uncomplicated with sure-footed results.

Ilan-

"You are a very good teacher!"

One year of ballet has brought a revelation to Ilan's daily life. She has many natural qualities for dancing, the most obvious is her natural grace in movement and her excellent physical proportions. The day will arrive when she is confident to trust herself without watching others.

Sun-

"Oh! I am not experienced yet!"

This comment is made whenever I remind her that she has been in class for over two years. With very good attendance, she demonstrates that we all have our unique manner of dealing with our fears and insecurities but I am also reminded that we cannot hide behind our work. We are the sum of our good efforts.

Ginny-

"Is it better?"

A beautician by trade, Ginny brought immediate artistic quality to the class. One can see that anything she does is

a work of beauty. She is an example of the need to take one's exercise routine seriously enough to make it a priority on the same day of the week. Best results occur that way.

Janet-

"I am a gypsy at heart!"

Indeed, the first time Janet appeared, I was sure a gypsy had joined the class. She had the gypsy soul and, on that day, the outfit to match. Since then, some four years later, the outfit has been replaced by proper class attire but the soul is still intact! Of course, her spirit for dancing is the root of her work and it has become more balanced by learning how to work correctly.

Jane T-

"Let me get this right!"

With the detailed mind of the engineer that she is, Jane has taken to ballet lessons with intense interest and forthright application. Over the years, she has found her center of movement and her sense of plié. She knows how balanced ballet lessons make her life and, as is the case in our work, continues to improve her movement quality with repetition.

Gail-

"I'll be getting leather shoes!"

An accomplished visual artist, Gail incorporates ballet lessons with meditation and yoga. Her approach is hands on and her straightforward effort rewards her within the time she can give to each endeavor. Again, ballet lessons provide an important facet to this artist's life. And, leather shoes provide a whole lot better support than canvas shoes do!

Maria-

"Grazie, Maestro!"

With love for the ballet and a niece who is a professional dancer, Maria decided to try ballet herself. She brings a flavor to her movements that indicates her appreciation for the classwork. She has steadily benefitted from her effort. Prego, Maria!

Carol M-

"Oh! I enjoy your lessons so much!"

As far as I know, Carol is the only singer in the class of so many. This fact is indicative of her approach to movement and to the grace she has developed through singing. She is "proceeding" beautifully and I like to think her consistent attendance is a large part of that.

Ting-

"I am always trying."

I hear this when I compliment Ting. Her natural ability is an asset that is not neglected by lack of effort. Her nature is to try and her results are indicative of her attendance. As is often the case, she brings her unique sense of grace to be refined.

Irina-

"I am not Elena!"

A mathematician with the grace of a dancer, Irina has been a class member for two years. I now know she is Irina but she looks like Elena, a former teacher of mine. Irina's confidence in taking the class has developed steadily and her natural feeling for dancing is always evident.

Ludmila-

"I am liking ballet lessons so much!"

Her Russian background is clearly the key to her understanding and love of the arts, ballet being one she practices. With Ludmila as a member of the class, I am reminded of the great educational system she comes out of and of how sustaining it is.

Cindy-

"I am not Stacy!"

Again, I mistake a name but not a back! Cindy had no prior training until she joined the class a couple of years ago. Now she is totally aware of what she is attempting and achieving lesson by lesson by lesson.

Barb P-

"Fantastic!"

A long time balletomane with many years of dance training, Barb was one of the first members of the class. Her consistency and interest in working in other exercise disciplines has benefitted her top priority: Dance!

Barbara B-

"Your combinations are the most musical I have ever danced."

An academic teacher, Barbara has a long history in ballet. She began training as a child. For most of her adult life she continued taking lessons because she loved it so. The continuous training has helped her to keep in touch with what she has been associated with for so long.

Carrolle-

"I feel so much better for learning ballet!"

Carrolle has come to the class as a retiree and has taken to the effort with consistency and a calm, steady enjoyment. She wants to learn more all the time and I think she is overjoyed to have found ballet at this point in her life.

Lisa-

"Well, yes when you have a great teacher...."

Commenting on my assessment of her natural ability and the improvement she has made, Lisa has made ballet class a priority. With only a total of one year of ballet lessons, Lisa has begun to find her center for moving and her confidence gets brighter by the lesson.

Alice-

"I'll be gone for three months!"

But she always comes back. Alice is a retired school teacher who has been a class member for many years. She also has an extensive ballet background, having studied most of her life. She encourages me, because with all her experience, she has adjusted well to my lessons and always makes me feel good about it.

Michael-

"Ballet has improved all my other activities!"

For Michael, a dentist, who was blessed with good physical qualities, ballet lessons improved his Karate and

Gymnastic activities. Interestingly, these other activities lacked the rudiments ballet offered. One could say he was starting backwards. However, he cut to the chase and not only learned quickly but applied what he learned immediately. It is clear that he can continue a full week of exercise scheduling until his body tells him to modify.

Carol C-

"Is this right?"

A more appropriate question there could not be. Carol is also a psychologist who found ballet in her adult years. Finding the "right" way is what we all seek and one senses that Carol finds it in all her endeavors. Carol has excellent attendance and that has supported her through physical trials she has endured outside her ballet training experience.

Carol and Ann-

"We love ballet!"

These two ladies are my Monday "specials." For a variety of reasons, mostly fun in other activities, they cannot make any other day for their ballet lesson. Their appreciation for the art form is of a very high order even though certain physical problems have forced Ann to stop taking lessons altogether.

Ellen G-

"I'll be back."

One of the really devoted members who is a school teacher and a club instructor as well. Obviously her schedule doesn't allow her attendance to be consistent, save holidays and summer vacations. Still, she maintains her condition and love for dance.

Mies-

"Thank you so much for your corrections!"

Mies came to the class with prior training and a large background in general folk dancing. She brought along her dedication. Her regard for ballet and the training it has provided her is paramount in her expression. As a school administrator, she has managed to get to class during the school year.

Maureen-

"Could you teach more?"

Though my schedule would not permit it, Maureen joined other classes and I think it is to her credit that she still gets to my lesson once a week even though she lives a good distance away. This is another fine example of determination and love of dance.

Michelle R-

"Thank you, Bob."

A ballroom dancing lawyer, Michelle has a very generous nature. I have seen her on the ballroom dance floor.
Her ballet training is evident. I would liked to have to
have seen her ballroom dancing before she began taking
ballet class!

Julia-

"I really love your teaching!"

A former dancer, Julia moved from California where
she gained wide experience owning her own dance school.
She is the only dance teacher in the class and has been able
to substitute teach for me on occasion. I feel my corrections are taking on a new life through her, as she hopefully
melds them into her own methods of teaching.

Helen M-

"I will be away again!"

Helen is away more than not. She and her husband are
in their retirement years and, for him, that means travel.
However, when I do have the opportunity to instruct her,
she shows her respect for ballet training in how she applies
the corrections and in her regret for having to leave us
"again."

Mikako-

"Thank you very much for everything."

She had no prior training but joined the class with utter sincerity and even greater hope that she would manage well in it. Her slow progress is indicative of the time she is able to put into the lessons in addition to the fact that she has found another creative outlet; she has recently become a mother.

Laurel-

"Could we do that on the left?"

A dancer's dancer, Laurel has a lot of feeling for dancing and a good deal of prior training. Her work needed to be centered and the rest was a "no-brainer." Her infectious spirit is a pleasure to experience.

Dea-

"It has been a very long time!"

Well, in dance terms that can be an assessment from a still rather young person. A large background of ballet training has really supported Dea's return to lessons. As a teacher in academia, she struggles with attendance but, at least in the summers, I see her regularly and we all enjoy her lovely and generous movement quality.

All of these people continue to take class. Their occupations and educations are varied and extensive. They range in age from twenty-five to eighty years. The class size has averaged forty students for a long time now.

For the multitude of others who have been a part of the classes over these years and given us a shorter time together, I know we all hope that they are taking lessons somewhere and feeling the physical and psychological benefits still.

Tendu en Avant en Plié

Making Ballet Class Approachable

I have often been asked to describe how I am thinking when I am instructing an adult ballet lesson. How do I do what I do and what is it that makes my instruction special to many people? I don't know precisely but I suspect we are talking about something that is a combination of several aspects.

Instead, I would like to go back to the fact that I began taking ballet lessons as an adult, albeit a young seventeen year-old adult. This plays nicely in my understanding of how adults become smitten with ballet training. I can remember well the feeling of elation and discovery in each and every one of my first ballet lessons. It is much like the feeling I have continually seen and heard about from the adult class members, especially those who are discovering ballet training for the very first time.

The common denominator present is the fact that we all love dance. Taking ballet lessons is the manner in which adults can have a close experience of the work and the feeling of wonder that it provides.

Instructing is and of itself an act of expression. It is that understanding which differentiates one instructor from another. I am an inclusive person. That means that I see others as a part of what I am doing in the lesson. I often ask the class members to partake in the instruction process by having them demonstrate the incorrect execution of a step for the benefit of the others in the class. They learn what it is that they need to do to improve the step and the others learn at the same time. This approach is less intimidating than being singled out for making an error.

My eye for detail has become very sharp and, as a result, I apparently miss very little when I am looking at an individual in a dance position. I know when a person is in a state of unbalance and/or physical stress and I feel that I have the tools to correct the situation. Experience is a good friend.

It is important to keep in mind that as we learn at an adult age, we will never catch up to those who have started as an adolescent. This is true in all aspects of learning, from piano to language to bicycle riding to swimming. Thus, repeated mistakes are common even after one has been corrected several times. The learning process takes longer for adults than it does for children.

At one of my son's piano recitals, when an adult student played very beautifully, I relayed my appreciation to the teacher. "Oh, but he will never catch up to your son Matthew's ability. He started too late." At times during my career, I have wondered what level of dancer I might have been had I started training earlier.

So it is with most of the adult ballet class population in general. Each may have wanted to dance more "seriously" or to have had a greater involvement. Whatever the case, I feel it is essential that the current experience in dance is positive and, hopefully, inspiring.

The term "approachable" at the heading of this chapter is reasonably apt for the adult who has taken the initiative to get into a dance lesson. He or she is addressing a fundamental need, one that should be received with dignity. My responsibility is to create an atmosphere of welcome and warmth, giving and taking away, while allowing the work to set the serious tone.

The beauty of repetitive work within a technique is that one really never tires of it. Particularly because of this fact, the instructor needs to be sensitive, on a lesson by lesson basis, of who is in front of him, how often he sees that person and how well that person appears to be. The work takes care of itself but in all other matters, we are our brother's keeper.

"All our spirits are welcome"

"*Music fires
imagination*"

Music

The very reason we are compelled to move – MUSIC!

Of the comments I have heard about my lessons, it is the inspiration of the music that has been the most remarked upon.

On every level and at all ages, humans are sent into a myriad of rhythmical movements when they hear music. Though the least complex of sounds, the human heart was Man's first experience with rhythm. It is also the steadiest and clearest of all meters.

Of the creative expressions that use music as a base, dancing is the most primitive. Indeed, Man first moved before he accomplished anything else. One easily imagines the primitive days with the sounds of bird and animal life, rain, thunder and waterfalls giving Man his first rhythmic sense from outside his body.

Dance instruction need not only be simple but the music chosen must also be basic in its rhythmical meter. Ballet class has the most basic meters in all dance instruction: square 2/4, 3/4 and 4/4 throughout the lesson. Of further interest is the manner in which the physical dynamic can accent the music even though the meter is not dynamic: this is the grated cheese that makes the pasta taste so good!

Not all ballet studios have pianos with pianists accompanying the teacher. With the exception of the professional ballet schools and companies, the vast majority of American dance schools train the future dancers of the country with the economical aid of the CD. For the most part, CDs suffice nicely.

Though there are hundreds of ballet CDs on the market, I, like many teachers, have yet to find one that satisfies my notion of what a ballet lesson's music should be; combination by combination, and for the overall musical development of the lesson. So, I have compiled custom-made CDs for my lessons, each one compiled from several other CDs. This, obviously, has much to do with the individual instructor's preferences for which music quality is appropriate for the instruction of a lesson. Inspiration is the sought after ingredient here. It is what can lift a combination from a sense of effort to the very special joy of dancing. Music, the dancer's keeper, is the raison d'etre of the lesson. I always feel that it is the music that keeps the lesson balanced.

Keeping perspective is key to maintaining the appreciation for the art form, teacher as well as student. If there is one thing that can easily run amok, it is the instructor loosing control of the class. This happens most often when the teacher loses interest, begins giving exercises that are too difficult for the class and loses perspective.

In order to keep the ambience of learning and giving present, I have garnered a few things about adults learning ballet that I would like to share for the benefit of all, instructor and student alike.

Arabesque à la Barre

Why, How and When

There was a time when many class members wanted extra work (can't the lesson be fifteen minutes longer?) private group classes after the regular lesson finished and, inevitably, private individual lessons. Occasionally, one asked if she could wear pointe shoes in the lesson and finally, several asked if they could have a choreographed work made for them.

All the above made perfect sense, given the nature of the class work and, indeed, for those who needed it, I did give private half-hour lessons. This made sense for the circumstance at hand, particularly if one needed to catch up or was having difficulties in class. For the most part, the private lessons continued for a set period of time.

My number one concern has always been safety and I am satisfied that we have not had injuries in the classes.

Additionally, the hour-long lesson given on alternate days of the week with a total of three lessons per week was what I deemed appropriate for the curriculum I developed. Time has proven the value of this plan.

There can be a tendency for adults to take their appreciation for the ballet lesson to another, somewhat dangerous level. Exceeding the regular adult ballet schedule can be injurious. It isn't long before their bodies inform them that they are overworking.

I advise people not to practice alone. Without the eye of an instructor, adults are even more likely than children to develop bad habits, and faster too! Adult muscle mass and strength are often liabilities here.

Though all adults who study ballet should be reminded that they are not being trained to be performers, the work in and of itself does present that illusion. It is, after all, the study of a performing art form. Still, I address this aspect in conversations outside the lesson whenever the opportunity arises. It is part of my work as an adult ballet instructor.

There are numerous reasons why most "would-be" dancers do not become dancers. Still, it is important to admit that it is alright to have missed the opportunity for the sake of the choices one did make. Most professional dancers begin their careers at the point when others begin their college educations. It is also alright not to have had the opportunity at all but to have the experience of learning ballet as an adult. And that encompasses just about everyone who takes the lessons.

The unusual example of one beginning late, putting all his eggs in one basket, going for it and having success at it is a tale others would not likely emulate. Most people tell me the risks would be too great. Thus, such an example is truly unusual, nothing else. As one who knows about doing just that, I was aware of the risks and took them.

The human spirit must soar, finding a way to live to the fullest for at least a part of life. Dancing is soaring in its most literal sense and dancers make a habit of soaring.

"In your own way, chance soaring."

"Beauty is
in the giving.
Giving of the
constructive kind"

A Summation/Revelation

When one plans to take a specific path and, indeed, designs a plan for that path, he is open to all the possibilities that are most likely to come from his plan.

I did not make a plan to become a successful and popular instructor of adult ballet. To be honest, I planned only to find a means to return to the physical and happy condition I had known as a dancer. This seemed a way to regain at least a portion of that condition. My objective achieved, I learned that helping others to be physically and psychologically happy was the greater result of my initial plan.

The response to my work and to my persona as an instructor has developed significantly since I began instructing adults at the Club in 1996. I had been successful in other teaching "forays" so I was comfortable instructing adult students. I have learned that the rewards of aging bring along the expertise garnered from having stayed with an endeavor long enough to become accomplished at it. Success follows. If you keep at it long enough you will reap the benefits of what you sow. Cliché as it may seem, if you put yourself out there, who knows what can become of you and what you are doing?

One does simplify and hone over time. That is what Man needs when working through life and that is what the students reconfirm each time they take a lesson. We all require a certain amount of repetition in order to feel accomplished. The age-old ballet technique, with its inherent repetition, could not have been a better choice for the adult-exercising public.

The act of instructing adults to become more capable of proprioception (the position of one's limbs) as a finite extension of the torso produces results that are often termed "revelatory." Often, after the two year mark in regular class attendance, I hear the remark that one has reached an "important understanding." That one has finally understood (put muscle to knowledge) what it was that was being taught all along. This repetitive comment has indicated to me that, on the average, it takes about that long for the mind/body learning process to kick in to the comfort zone. Children take on the experience of "feeling" what it is they are being taught instantaneously, albeit unrefined.

This is in line with other learning processes that adults experience, i.e. new languages, career changes, etc. Incorporating the study of a physical artform as opposed to a solely cerebral learning experience, one can appreciate the high degree of benefit and satisfaction the learner feels from having spent the consistent effort at getting to the "revelation." This turning point in training is important for several reasons. First, it reflects the interest and commitment made to date. Second, it brings the sense of general satisfaction with the lessons to a new level and, finally, it frees the person for the most rewarding stage of the entire ballet class experience: dancing with technique.

From this point forward, it is clear that the training will be applied in one degree or another to all of the learner's physical movements. One walks, sits and moves in an overall enhanced manner. One experiences new muscular control while doing the most mundane task. One is moving with a degree of grace all the time; moving more easily and feeling better for it.

Though we may not become an adult ballet-trained nation as we have with other physical fitness forms, I am seeing more people who show some degree of dance training in their carriage and overall deportment. They are not getting that from the Elliptical Stair-master machine.

We are also seeing the multitudes of dance students, who after going on to college, etc., and not pursuing professional dance careers, return to ballet class as young adults. In them we see a different revelation, one that harks back to something they knew very well and are once again becoming physically and psychologically reacquainted with. They are the leaders of the future adult ballet class population.

The Instructor Instructs

The Instructor Instructs

. Instruct the focus positions from the very
  BEGINNING: tendu en avant, gaze tilted over
  extended hand at the side- tendu á la seconde,
  eyes forward- tendu derrière, gaze tilted toward
  inside of extended palm.

. In order to not lock the ankle or over stiffen the
  instep, POINT THE TOE, NOT THE FOOT.

. Stretch the TOES and FINGERS when
  initiating movement with the limbs.

. Use the floor when moving from a closed
  position to an open position and visa versa.
  MAKE NOISE WITH YOUR FOOT.

. Rising movements go DOWN, bending movements go UP.

. Movement BEGINS with the port de bras and is COMPLEMENTED by the line of the legs.

. In traveling combinations, LOOK first, then begin movement with arms leading legs.

. Take your BACK to each new position.

Using the front of the room (Mirror) as #1, count clockwise around the room. You will have even numbers for the corners and odd numbers for the walls.

When instructing the eight positions of the body, the order I use is:

Croisé en avant (body 8, gaze 2)
En avant (body and gaze above eye level 1)
Effacé (body 2, gaze 8)
Écarté en avant (body 8, gaze 2)
À la seconde (body and gaze above eye level 1)
Épaulé (body 8, gaze 2)
Derrière (body and gaze above eye level 1)
Croisé Derrière (body 2, gaze 8)
The ninth body position is écarté derrière

All begin with fingers passing through first port de bras.

The five arabesques begin with the body facing corner eight, standing in third position, and the gaze tilted toward corner two. First arabesque begins through passé.

The pas de bourrée between the second and third arabesque moves toward corner six with a proper second position executed in the pas de bourrée.

Stepping into the third arabesque from the deep demi-plié at the end of the pas de bourrée, one then moves directly into fourth arabesque and onto fifth arabesque (in plié) to pas de bourrée à la seconde, changing the starting position now to the left side, body facing corner two.

Moving on to the port de bras, we do them in chronological order using plié at the end of third and plié for both feet in fourth position (not the lunge fourth) for the sixth port de bras.

Balancé (en écarté, à la seconde, devant, derrière, en tournant and en place), tombé pas de bourrée, relevé, pirouette preparations before turning en dehors and en dedans, small temps levé and changement, glissade and petit jeté comprise the center work plan culminating in chaînés and piqué turns from the corner or the grand allegro which can include pas de couru, pas de chats and tombé pas de bourrée glissade jeté.

Sample Beginner Lesson

The exercises of Adult Beginner Ballet Class should be devoid of force in any position. Emphasis should be on breathing. Do not begin the class without using the floor work explained on page 5 (Lesson) of this book.

After completing the beginning floor work, the students stand facing the BARRE:

TENDU and DEMI-PLIÉ-
Facing the barre in first position, shoulders aligned over hips and feet with elbows slightly in front of waist (be sure elbows are slightly bent). In slow 2/4 time, do tendu à la seconde three times finishing in a two count demi plié-right and left. End exercise with a two count demi plié into direct relevé for two counts, repeat three times finishing in demi plié.

Throughout the exercise, caution class about alignment with emphasis on the importance of standing on the feet with weight distributed equally. This is the time to give the direction to have all five toes firmly planted on the floor, as well as feeling this with the weight on only one foot while the other foot is in tendu position. One should always feel as though one could rise onto the ball of the foot so as to assure that the weight does not drop back to the heel as it is wont to do.

A helpful correction for plié is to feel the energy in the body rising while the movement is going lower, with the reverse being true of the relevé. This is particularly helpful for finding balance on relevé in that one feels connected to the floor even though the movement to get there is upward.

Repeat the same exercise with the left hand on the barre and then with the right hand on the barre. It is important here to notice that the hand on the barre is resting with the palm over the barre and the position of the hand is in front of the waist. Feel the barre with all five fingers of which the thumb is placed over the barre (this will help the elbow not to rise upward).

DÉGAGÉ-
With the left hand on the barre, move the right leg to tendu in the second position and lift the foot slightly off the floor (dégagé) placing it back to the floor and close in first position. Repeat four times followed by eight times in full dégagé (without stopping to lift the foot from the floor initially). Finish with demi plié and relevé three times. End in plié from the last relevé. Remind students to go up on the plié and down on the relevé. Watch for forward

placement in the closing of the stance when the students straighten the legs after plié. This is often where the weight shifts backwards and the alignment again weakens.

ROND DE JAMBE-
With the students in first position facing the barre with relaxed elbows in front of the waist, hands on the barre, make the shape of the upper case letter "D" with the right foot first (semi-circle passing through first position each time). Because we are rotating the turned-over leg shape, we now have a better feeling of only using the muscles we need and not involving the hips to do the movement.

Do four ronde jambe en dehors and four en dedans, stopping in positions en avant, à la seconde and derrière. Demi plié to relevé ending with demi plié. Check alignment as legs straighten.

FRAPPÉ-
The frappé requires a quick attack from the metatarsal. In this action the alignment can easily revert to the heel. Articulation of the metatarsal is required. In first position with the left hand on the barre, pick up the heel leaving the ball of the foot on the floor. While pressing down onto the ball of the foot, pick up the toes off the floor. Reverse the action to place the foot back onto the floor. Repeat three times with the foot resting on the left ankle in sur le coup de pied position on the fourth time. Next, strike the floor with the ball of the foot ending in dégagé position en avant. Continue to the à la seconde position and the derrière position and finally to the à la seconde position again. Finish with seven frappé à la seconde and demi plié in third position. Straighten legs without settling on heels. Repeat.

GRANDE BATTEMENT-

Beginning with the back to the barre in first position, hands along the barre with relaxed elbows (one needs to be close to the barre without touching the hips to the barre) tendu the right foot en avant, lift to dégagé, return to tendu and close back to first position three times. On the fourth time do full grande battement brushing the floor on the way up and carrying the leg back to first position. Repeat with the left leg. In the same position, do the same combination à la seconde. Lastly, facing the barre (one needs to be far enough from the barre so that the elbows are slightly in front of the waist) repeat the combination derrière but do not repeat á la seconde.

CENTER WORK

PORT DE BRAS / TEMPS LIÉ-

The studio has four walls and four corners. Facing the front wall (#1) move to the right counting all corners and walls. You will finish with #8. Walls are numbered 1,3,5 and 7. Corners are numbered 2,4,6, and 8. Beginner adults stand in third position and begin with body in croisé position, right foot front facing corner #8.

	front	
8	wall 1	2
7		3
6	5	4

In port de bras, the head is always relaxed over the front foot.

First port de bras keeps the hands well below the apex of the chest bone, the hands led by the stretch in the finger tips. Opening fully to the second position without leaning backward and closing to bras bas position by relaxing the elbows. The fingers finish with the pinky finger resting lightly on the middle of the thigh. Proceed to the second port de bras and finish with third port de bras and demi-plié to tendu écarté derrière, closing behind to begin the other side. Now the student is facing corner #2.

For temps lié, facing #1 in first position, tendu à la seconde five times. On the sixth tendu, bend both knees in second position to fully change the weight to the other foot. Finish in first position. The arms perform first port de bras in temps lié. Repeat to the other side.

BALANCÉ / TOMBÉ PAS DE BOURRÉE-

Balancé or waltz step requires a clear sense of tombé (falling) onto the first step of the three-step waltz. Informing the class that the accent in a waltz is on the first note of the measure helps them with the physicality of this step. Beginning with the right foot from third position croisé (facing corner #8) tombé to the side on the right foot, bring the left foot directly behind and almost touching the right foot, piqué on the left foot for weight change finishing with the right foot placing where it was in the tombé. Repeat immediately to the left, always leading the movement with the gaze in the direction one is going. Arms are relaxed going in the direction of the movement without over crossing the center of the body.

Balancé six times, ending with tombé pas de bourrée. Again accent the tombé for the pas de bourrée and inform that the second foot in this step crosses behind as one is literally dancing sideways. Use first port de bras to do this step. Repeat to the left.

SAUT / RÉVÉRENCE-

Six small sauts in first position facing the front (#1). Finish with first port de bras. Repeat this three times (watch that the alignment does not go backward as the body leaves the floor). On the fourth time, simply do first port de bras again, ramassé (bending forward as if to pick something up from the floor) leading with the relaxed head movement and recover to the upright alignment with the arms overhead leading the recovery. Repeat all in second position returning back to first position at the end of the music.

Finish the class with révérence. Improvise a short révérence, to an adagio tempo, for the class to follow. Use port de bras, tendus, ramassé with grande révérence, plié and small walking steps in a circle.

Glossary of Basic Ballet Terms

adagio-   Slow, sustained movements or exercises

à la seconde-   Second position

allegro-   Any sequence of steps done to a fast
                  tempo

arabesque-   One leg extended back, knee straight,
                  toe pointed

balancé-   A step usually in 3/4 time

barre-   A hand rail which is intended to
                  support the dancer during exercises

cambré-   Arching of the body from the waist, to
                  the side or backward

chaînés-	Repeated short turns
changement-	A change of foot position during a jump
croisé-	A body pose in which the dancer stands at an angle to the spectator with legs crossed
dégagé-	Extending the foot off the floor with pointed toe
demi-	A movement or pose executed in only part of full strength
derrière-	In back of
développé-	A movement in which the working leg is slowly raised and extended
écarté-	A pose in which the body is at an oblique angle to the spectator, and one leg is extended in the same diagonal line
effacé-	A pose in which the body is at an angle to the spectator with one leg extended away from the body, not crossing
en avant-	In a forward direction

en dedans-	This phrase indicates that the working leg moves in an inward position
en dehors-	This phrase indicates that the working leg moves in an outward position
épaulé-	A pose in which one shoulder is forward and the head is turned in the same direction
en place-	Standing in place
en tournant-	Turning to the other side
frappé-	An exercise starting in second position, in which the working foot first beats the ankle of the supporting leg, and then strikes the floor in returning to second position
glisssade-	A movement characterized by gliding
grand battement-	An exercise in which the working leg is raised to 90 degrees, and lowered
pas de bourrée-	Repetitive movement covering the ground in in any direction

pas de chats-	A cat-like step
pas de couru-	A running step
petit jeté-	Small jumps alternating feet en place.
piqué-	A step on half-toe
pirouette-	A completed turn on one leg in which the arm movement gives momentum
plié-	Bending the knees, while the legs are well turned out, with weight equally distributed on both feet
ramassé-	bending forward, as in picking something up
relevé-	A movement in which the dancer rises to a position on demi-point
révérence-	A bow or curtsy
rond de jambe-	A circular motion of one leg inward or outward
saut-	A jump

temps levé-	A hop from one foot with the other foot raised in any direction
temps lié-	A connected movement, changing from one foot to another
tendu-	A phrase to indicate that the working leg is held or stretched
tombé-	Shifting weight to a different position

Appreciation

To the Club management and staff who, over the years, have been warmly supportive of my interest in bringing ballet lessons into their arena, I am very grateful. To my wife, ballerina Linda DiBona, for her continued support as she observes her dancing partner becoming a writer, I am always appreciative. To Phil Schaffer for his detailed insight into editing this manuscript, I am indebted. I thank Shayna Loeffler for the enthusiasm and talent she brings to designing and for her beautiful rendering of this book. Finally, for all of you who have, over the years, ventured into "Studio B" every Monday, Wednesday or Friday, giving so fully to our combined effort, I thank you for enhancing my own dance experience.

ROBERT BRASSEL's extensive ballet career spanned twenty-five years, encompassed travel to thirty countries on five continents and was interrupted during the Vietnam War for service to his country. He was a charter member of the City Center Joffrey Ballet and danced for four years with American Ballet Theatre before spending the remainder of his career performing internationally.

His teaching experience began in his own Academy, opened in 1981, and continued through a career change into the corporate world of Insurance. Mr. Brassel is credited with bringing the professional dance world the first disability insurance policy in 1990 as well as Beginner Adult Ballet Lessons to the Health Club industry in 1996. He is the subject and author of *Always a Dancer*, a memoir published in 2006.

Printed in Great Britain
by Amazon

54142097R00066